Wonderful ways to prepare

COCKTAILS & MIXED DRINKS

by JO ANN SHIRLEY

Wonderful ways to prepare

COCKTAILS & MIXED DRINKS

PLAYMORE INC. NEW YORK USA
UNDER ARRANGEMENT WITH
WALDMAN PUBLISHING CORP.

AYERS & JAMES
SYDNEY AUSTRALIA

STAFFORD PEMBERTON PUBLISHING
KNUTSFORD UNITED KINGDOM

FIRST PUBLISHED 1979

PUBLISHED IN THE USA
BY PLAYMORE INC.
UNDER ARRANGEMENT WITH
WALDMAN PUBLISHING CORP.

PUBLISHED IN AUSTRALIA
BY AYERS & JAMES
CROWS NEST. AUSTRALIA

PUBLISHED IN THE UNITED KINGDOM
BY STAFFORD PEMBERTON PUBLISHING
KNUTSFORD CHESHIRE

COPYRIGHT © 1979
AYERS & JAMES
5 ALEXANDER STREET
CROWS NEST   N.S.W. AUSTRALIA

ISBN 0 86908 161 6

PRINTED IN CANADA

Contents

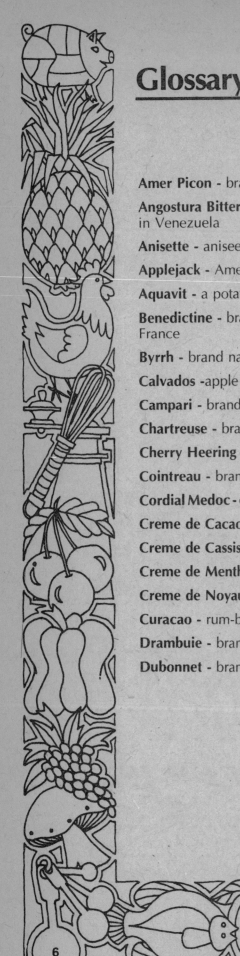

Glossary

Amer Picon - brand name of a French aperitif

Angostura Bitters - brand name of bitters which comes from the village of Angostura in Venezuela

Anisette - aniseed-flavored liqueur

Applejack - American term for apple brandy

Aquavit - a potato-based liqueur from Scandinavia flavored with caraway seeds

Benedictine - brandy-based liqueur originated by the Benedictine order of monks in France

Byrrh - brand name of a French aperitif

Calvados - apple brandy from Normandy in France

Campari - brand name of an Italian aperitif

Chartreuse - brand name of a French liqueur either green or yellow in color

Cherry Heering - brand name of a cherry-flavored liqueur

Cointreau - brand name of an orange-flavored liqueur

Cordial Medoc - chocolate-flavored French liqueur made in Bordeaux. Dark red in color.

Creme de Cacao - a chocolate-flavored liqueur

Creme de Cassis - French blackcurrant liqueur

Creme de Menthe - peppermint-flavored liqueur either green or white in color

Creme de Noyaux - brandy-based liqueur flavored with apricot and peach kernels

Curacao - rum-based liqueur flavored with orange peel

Drambuie - brand name of whisky-based liqueur from Scotland

Dubonnet - brand name of a French aperitif

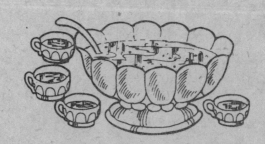

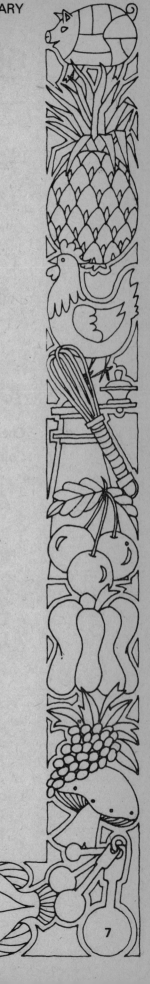

Fino Sherry - a pale dry sherry

Grand Marnier - brand name of an orange-flavored liqueur

Grenadine - a pomegranate-flavored syrup

Kirsch (or Kirschwasser) - a colorless cherry brandy

Kummel - a German liqueur flavored with aniseed and cumin

Lillet - brand name of a French aperitif

Madeira - a fortified wine from the island of Madeira

Maraschino Liqueur - a liqueur flavored with fruit kernels

Marsala - an Italian dessert wine

Orgeat - a flavoring made of almonds, sugar, orange-flavored water and brandy

Ouzo - an aniseed-flavored Greek liqueur

Pernod - a French aniseed-flavored aperitif

Pisco Brandy - a brandy from Peru

Prunelle - a French blackthorn (sloe)-flavored liqueur

Sake - Japanese rice wine

Slivovitz - a plum brandy from middle Europe

Sloe gin - a gin flavored with sloe (blackthorn)

Southern Comfort - brandy and bourbon based American liqueur

Strega - brand name of Italian liqueur

Triple Sec - orange-flavored liqueur

Aperitifs

Americano

1½ oz (45 ml) Campari
1½ oz (45 ml) sweet vermouth
lemon peel
soda water

Pour the Campari and sweet vermouth over ice in a chilled glass. Stir well. Twist the lemon peel over the glass then drop it in. Add a little soda water and serve.

Amer Picon Cocktail

1½ oz (45 ml) Amer Picon
1½ oz (15 ml) lemon juice
soda water
1 slice lemon

Pour Amer Picon and lemon juice into a glass over ice cubes. Add a little soda and stir. Top with lemon slice.

Amer Picon and Cognac

1½ oz (45 ml) Amer Picon
¼ teaspoon grenadine
soda water
15 ml (½ oz) cognac
lemon peel

Pour the Amer Picon and grenadine into a chilled glass over ice. Add a little soda water. Carefully pour on the cognac so it floats on the top. Twist the lemon peel over the glass, then drop it in.

Campari Cocktail

1 oz (30 ml) Campari
1 oz (30 ml) gin
1 oz (30 ml) dry vermouth
lemon peel

Stir the Campari, gin and vermouth with ice. Strain into a chilled glass. Twist the lemon peel above the glass, then drop it in.

Campari and Gin

1½ oz (45 ml) Campari
1½ oz (45 ml) gin
orange peel

Stir the Campari and gin with ice. Strain into a chilled glass over ice cubes. Twist the orange peel over the glass, then drop it in.

Campari and Soda

1½ oz (45 ml) Campari
soda water
half slice of orange

Pour the Campari into a glass filled with ice. Add amount of soda desired (not too much) and drop in the orange slice. Stir well.

Campari and Vodka

1 oz (30 ml) Campari
1 oz (30 ml) vodka
1 oz (30 ml) orange juice

Pour the Campari, vodka and orange juice into a cocktail shaker with ice. Shake well, then strain into a chilled glass.

Dubonnet Aperitif

1 oz (30 ml) Dubonnet
½ oz (15 ml) Amer Picon
½ oz (15 ml) Cointreau
½ oz (15 ml) lemon juice
1 slice lemon

Pour the Dubonnet, Amer Picon, Cointreau and lemon juice into a cocktail shaker with ice. Shake well. Strain into a chilled glass over ice. Garnish with lemon slice.

Dubonnet Cocktail

1½ oz (45 ml) Dubonnet
1½ oz (45 ml) gin
lemon peel

Stir the Dubonnet and gin with ice, then strain into a chilled glass. Twist the lemon peel above the glass, then drop it in.

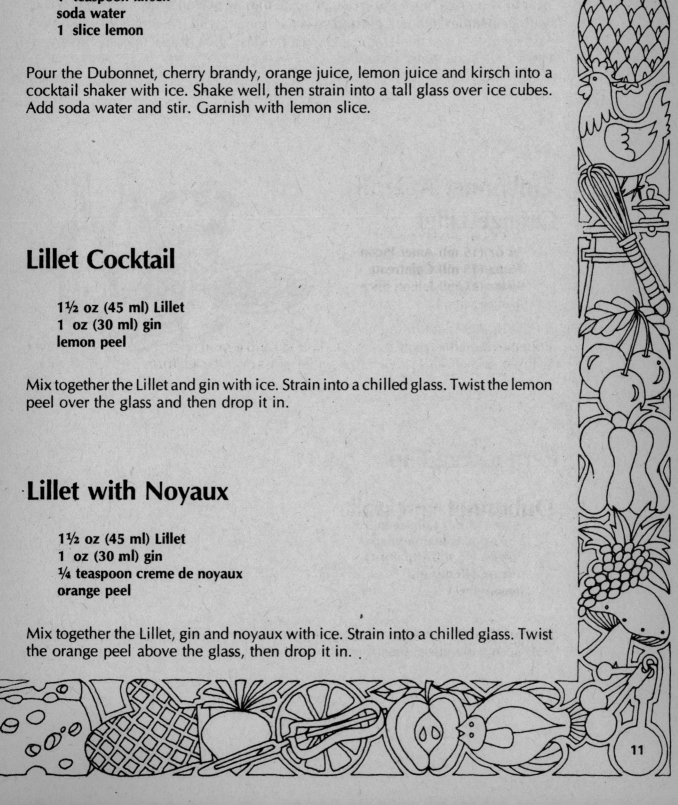

Dubonnet Fizz

1 oz (30 ml) Dubonnet
1 oz (30 ml) cherry brandy
1 oz (30 ml) orange juice
½ oz (15 ml) lemon juice
1 teaspoon kirsch
soda water
1 slice lemon

Pour the Dubonnet, cherry brandy, orange juice, lemon juice and kirsch into a cocktail shaker with ice. Shake well, then strain into a tall glass over ice cubes. Add soda water and stir. Garnish with lemon slice.

Lillet Cocktail

1½ oz (45 ml) Lillet
1 oz (30 ml) gin
lemon peel

Mix together the Lillet and gin with ice. Strain into a chilled glass. Twist the lemon peel over the glass and then drop it in.

Lillet with Noyaux

1½ oz (45 ml) Lillet
1 oz (30 ml) gin
¼ teaspoon creme de noyaux
orange peel

Mix together the Lillet, gin and noyaux with ice. Strain into a chilled glass. Twist the orange peel above the glass, then drop it in.

Negroni

1 oz (30 ml) Campari
1 oz (30 ml) gin
1 oz (30 ml) sweet vermouth
lemon peel

Mix together the Campari, gin and sweet vermouth with ice. Strain into a chilled glass over ice. Twist the lemon peel over the glass, then drop it in. May be served with a little soda water if desired.

Orange Lillet

3 oz (90 ml) Lillet
1 slice orange

Put the orange slice in the glass and pour the Lillet over it.

Pernod Egg Flip

1 oz (30 ml) Pernod
½ oz (15 ml) Cointreau
2 teaspoons lemon juice
1 egg
1 teaspoon sugar
nutmeg

Mix together the Pernod, Cointreau, lemon juice, egg and sugar in a cocktail shaker. Shake well and pour into a chilled glass. Sprinkle with nutmeg.

Suissesse

1½ oz (45 ml) Pernod
½ oz (15 ml) anisette
1½ teaspoons cream
½ egg white

Pour all the ingredients into a cocktail shaker with ice. Shake vigorously, then strain into a chilled glass.

Tiger Tail

4 oz (125 ml) fresh orange juice
1½ oz (45 ml) Pernod
1 slice lemon

Pour the orange juice and Pernod into a tall glass filled with crushed ice. Stir well. Garnish with lemon slice.

Bourbon Based Drinks

Bourbon Cocktail

1½ oz (45 ml) bourbon
½ oz (15 ml) dry vermouth
2 teaspoons creme de cassis
2 teaspoons lemon juice

Pour all the ingredients into a cocktail shaker with ice. Shake well, then strain into a chilled glass.

Bourbon Daisy

1½ oz (45 ml) bourbon
½ oz (15 ml) lemon juice
1 teaspoon grenadine
soda water
2 teaspoons Southern
    Comfort
½ slice orange
1 pineapple cube

Pour the bourbon, lemon juice and grenadine into a cocktail shaker with ice. Shake well, then strain into a tall glass over ice cubes. Add a little soda water and stir. Carefully pour on the Southern Comfort so it floats on top. Garnish with orange slice and pineapple cube.

Deep South

1½ oz (45 ml) bourbon
½ oz (15 ml) lemon juice
½ oz (15 ml) pineapple juice
¾ teaspoon maraschino
    liqueur

Pour all the ingredients into a cocktail shaker with ice. Shake well, then strain into a chilled sugar-frosted glass. (Wet the rim of the glass with maraschino liqueur and dip it in sugar.)

Hot Eggnog

1 egg
pinch of salt
1¼ tablespoons sugar
6 oz (165 ml) hot milk
60 ml (2 oz) bourbon
nutmeg

Beat the egg very well with the salt. Add the sugar and beat some more. Slowly add the hot milk, beating constantly. Beat in the bourbon and pour into a mug. Sprinkle on a little nutmeg.

Hot Toddy

1 teaspoon sugar
3 whole cloves
1 inch (2½ cm) cinnamon
   stick

1 slice lemon
2 oz (60 ml) boiling water
2 oz (60 ml) hot bourbon
nutmeg

Put the sugar, cloves, cinnamon stick and lemon into a mug. Pour on the boiling water and allow to stand for five minutes. Add the hot bourbon and stir. Sprinkle on a little nutmeg.

Mint Julep

10 mint leaves
1 teaspoon sugar
3 teaspoons water
2½ oz (75 ml) bourbon
6 mint leaves

Tear the ten mint leaves into quarters and put into a tall glass with the sugar and water. Crush the mint leaves while stirring to dissolve the sugar. Fill the glass with crushed ice and add the bourbon. Stir well. Tear the mint leaves in half and place on top of the ice.

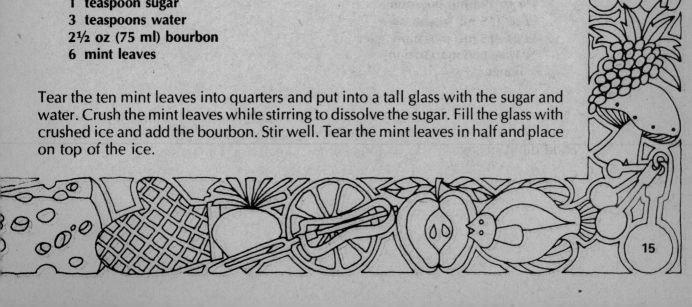

Rocky Mountain

1 oz (30 ml) bourbon
1 oz (30 ml) dry vermouth
2 teaspoons blackberry
   liqueur
2 teaspoons lemon juice
1 dash Angostura bitters
lemon peel

Pour the bourbon, vermouth, blackberry liqueur, lemon juice and bitters into a cocktail shaker with ice. Shake well, then strain into a chilled glass. Twist the lemon peel above the glass and drop it in.

Sweet Adelaide

¾ teaspoon sugar
1 dash Angostura bitters
soda water
1 oz (30 ml) bourbon

1 oz (30 ml) light rum
½ oz (15 ml) sweet vermouth
1 slice orange

Put the sugar, bitters and a little soda water into a glass. Stir until the sugar dissolves. Add the bourbon, rum, vermouth and a few ice cubes. Stir well. Add a little more soda water and garnish with orange slice.

Venetian Dream

1 oz (30 ml) bourbon
1 oz (30 ml) cognac
1 tablespoon Benedictine
1 oz (30 ml) orange juice
½ oz (15 ml) lemon juice
soda water
½ orange slice
1 lemon slice

Pour the bourbon, cognac, Benedictine, orange juice and lemon juice into a cocktail shaker with ice. Shake well, then strain into a tall glass over ice cubes. Add a little soda and stir. Garnish with orange and lemon slices.

Brandy Based Drinks

Apple Bitter

2 oz (60 ml) apple brandy
  (calvados or applejack)
2 dashes Angostura bitters
soda water
lemon peel

Pour the brandy and bitters into a glass filled with crushed ice. Add a little soda and mix well. Twist the lemon peel above the glass, then drop it in.

Apple Blossom

1½ oz (45 ml) apple brandy
  (calvados or applejack)
1 oz (30 ml) apple juice
½ oz (15 ml) lemon juice

1 teaspoon maple syrup
⅓ cup crushed ice
1 slice lemon

Put all the ingredients except the lemon slice into an electric blender. Whirl for 15 seconds. Pour into a chilled glass and garnish with lemon slice.

Apple Brandy Collins

    2 oz (60 ml) apple brandy
       (calvados or applejack)
    1 teaspoon sugar
    1 oz (30 ml) lemon juice
    2 dashes orange bitters
    soda water
    1 slice lemon

Put the apple brandy, sugar, lemon juice and bitters into a cocktail shaker. Strain into a tall glass over ice cubes. Add a little soda and stir well. Garnish with a lemon slice.

Apple Brandy Cooler

    2 oz (60 ml) brandy
    1 oz (30 ml) light rum
    3 oz (90 ml) apple juice
    ½ oz (15 ml) lemon juice
    1 teaspoon dark rum
    1 slice lemon

Pour the brandy, light rum, apple juice, lemon juice and dark rum into a cocktail shaker with ice. Shake well, then strain into a tall glass. Fill with ice and garnish with a slice of lemon.

Apple-Dubonnet

    1 oz (30 ml) apple brandy
       (calvados or applejack)
    1 oz (30 ml) Dubonnet
    1 slice lemon

Stir the brandy and Dubonnet together with ice. Strain into a chilled glass over ice cubes. Garnish with slice of lemon.

Apple Manhattan

2 oz (60 ml) apple brandy
(calvados or applejack)
1 oz (30 ml) sweet vermouth
1 dash orange bitters
1 maraschino cherry

Stir the brandy, vermouth and bitters with ice. Strain into a chilled glass and garnish with the cherry.

Apple Sidecar

1 oz (30 ml) apple brandy
(calvados or applejack)
1 oz (30 ml) Cointreau
1 oz (30 ml) lemon juice

Pour the brandy, Cointreau and lemon juice into a cocktail shaker with ice. Shake well, then strain into a chilled glass.

Apple Sour

2 oz (60 ml) apple brandy
(calvados or applejack)
½ oz (15 ml) lemon juice
1 teaspoon sugar
½ slice lemon

Put the brandy, lemon juice and sugar into a cocktail shaker with ice. Shake well, then strain into a chilled glass. Garnish with lemon slice.

Bombay

1 oz (30 ml) brandy
½ oz (15 ml) dry vermouth
½ oz (15 ml) sweet vermouth
½ teaspoon curacao
½ teaspoon Pernod
1 slice peach

Put the brandy, dry vermouth, sweet vermouth, curacao and Pernod into a cocktail shaker with ice. Shake well, then strain into a chilled glass. Garnish with a slice of peach.

Brandafino

1½ oz (45 ml) brandy
½ oz (15 ml) fino sherry
½ oz (15 ml) Drambuie
½ slice orange
lemon peel

Pour the brandy, fino sherry and Drambuie into a cocktail shaker with ice. Shake well, then strain into a chilled glass over ice cubes. Garnish with the orange slice. Twist the lemon peel over the glass, then drop it in.

Brandini

1½ oz (45 ml) brandy
1 oz (30 ml) gin
1 teaspoon dry vermouth
lemon peel

Mix the brandy, gin and vermouth with ice. Strain into a chilled glass. Twist the lemon peel above the glass, then drop it in.

Brandy Alexander

1 oz (30 ml) brandy
1 oz (30 ml) creme de cacao
1 oz (30 ml) cream
nutmeg

Pour the brandy, creme de cacao and cream into a cocktail shaker. Shake well, then strain into a chilled glass. Sprinkle with nutmeg.

Brandied Apricot

1½ oz (45 ml) brandy
½ oz (15 ml)
apricot-flavored brandy
½ oz (15 ml) lemon juice
lemon peel

Pour brandy, apricot-flavored brandy and lemon juice into a cocktail shaker. Shake well, then strain into a chilled sugar-frosted glass. Twist lemon peel over the glass, then drop it in.

Brandy and Cassis

2 oz (60 ml) brandy
1 oz (30 ml) lemon juice
2 teaspoons creme de cassis
lemon peel

Pour the brandy, lemon juice and creme de cassis into a cocktail shaker with ice. Shake well, then strain into a chilled glass. Twist the lemon peel above the glass, then drop it in.

Brandy Classic

1½ oz (45 ml) brandy
½ oz (15 ml) lemon juice
1½ teaspoons maraschino
    liqueur
1½ teaspoons curacao

Pour all the ingredients into a cocktail shaker with ice. Shake well, then strain into a chilled glass.

Brandy Cobbler

1½ oz (45 ml) brandy
½ oz (15 ml) curacao
½ oz (15 ml) lemon juice
1¼ teaspoons sugar
1 teaspoon kirsch
1 chunk pineapple

Fill a tall glass with crushed ice and add the brandy, curacao, lemon juice, sugar and kirsch. Stir well. Garnish with chunk of pineapple.

Brandy Crusta

2 oz (60 ml) brandy
½ oz (15 ml) curacao
1½ teaspoons lemon juice
1 dash bitters

1 teaspoon maraschino
   liqueur
lemon peel
maraschino cherry

Pour the brandy, curacao, lemon juice, bitters and maraschino liqueur into a cocktail shaker with ice. Shake well, then strain into a sugar-frosted glass filled with crushed ice. Garnish with lemon peel and cherry.

Brandy Frappe

1 oz (30 ml) brandy
2 teaspoons creme de noyaux
½ oz (15 ml)
   apricot-flavored brandy

Mix together the brandy, creme de noyaux and apricot-flavored brandy. Pour into a glass filled with crushed ice.

Brandy and Lemon Juice

2 oz (60 ml) brandy
½ oz (15 ml) lemon juice
½ teaspoon grenadine

Pour the brandy, lemon juice and grenadine into a cocktail shaker with ice. Shake well, then strain into a chilled glass.

Brandy Manhattan

2 oz (60 ml) brandy
½ oz (15 ml) sweet vermouth
1 dash bitters
1 maraschino cherry

Stir the brandy, vermouth and bitters with ice. Strain into a chilled glass. Garnish with the maraschino cherry.

Brandy Mist

2 oz (60 ml) brandy
crushed ice

Pour the brandy into a glass filled with finely crushed ice.

Brandy Punch

2 quarts dry white wine
2 bottles brandy
1 cup (250 ml) strong tea, brewed with 12 whole cloves and 3 cinnamon sticks
2 cups (500 ml) soda water

Mix all the ingredients together and pour into a punch bowl over a large block of ice.

Brandy Sour

2 oz (60 ml) brandy
½ oz (15 ml) orange juice
½ oz (15 ml) lemon juice
½ teaspoon sugar
½ slice lemon
1 maraschino cherry

Mix together the brandy, orange juice, lemon juice and sugar in a cocktail shaker with ice. Shake well, then strain into a chilled glass. Garnish with lemon slice and maraschino cherry.

Byrrh Cocktail

1½ oz (45 ml) Byrrh
1½ oz (45 ml) gin
lemon peel

Mix the Byrrh and the gin with ice. Strain into a chilled glass. Twist the lemon peel over the glass, then drop it in.

Byrrh Cooler

2 oz (60 ml) Byrrh
½ oz (15 ml) creme de cassis
soda water
1 slice lemon

Pour Byrrh and creme de cassis over ice in a tall glass. Add a little soda water and stir. Garnish with the lemon slice.

Champagne Soda

1 teaspoon sugar
1 dash Angostura bitters
1½ teaspoons brandy
1 teaspoon kirsch
champagne
lemon sherbet

Put the sugar, bitters, brandy and kirsch into a tall glass and stir until the sugar dissolves. Fill almost to the top with champagne. Float a scoop of lemon sherbet on top.

Cherbourg

1 oz (30 ml) brandy
½ oz (15 ml) lemon juice
½ oz (15 ml) apple brandy
½ oz (15 ml) Triple Sec

Pour all the ingredients into a cocktail shaker with ice. Shake well, then strain into a chilled glass.

Cognac Cream

2 oz (60 ml) cognac
2 oz (60 ml) cream
3 oz (90 ml) milk
½ oz (15 ml) grenadine
nutmeg

Pour the cognac, cream, milk and grenadine into a cocktail shaker with ice. Shake well, then strain into a tall glass over ice cubes. Sprinkle with nutmeg.

Cognac Egg Flip

1½ oz (45 ml) cognac
1 oz (30 ml) tawny port
1 egg
1¼ teaspoons sugar
nutmeg

Pour the cognac, port, egg and sugar into a cocktail shaker with ice. Shake very well, then strain into a chilled glass. Sprinkle with nutmeg.

Creme de Menthe and Brandy Cooler

1½ teaspoons creme de
   menthe
1½ oz (45 ml) brandy
½ oz (15 ml) lemon juice
ginger ale
3 seedless green grapes

Pour the creme de menthe, brandy and lemon juice into a cocktail shaker with ice. Shake well, then strain into a tall glass over ice cubes. Add a little ginger ale and stir. Garnish with grapes.

Cuban Apple

1½ oz (45 ml) apple brandy
    (calvados or applejack)
1 oz (30 ml) light rum
½ oz (15 ml) lime juice
1½ teaspoons orgeat
1 slice lime

Pour the apple brandy, rum, lime juice and orgeat into a cocktail shaker with ice. Shake well, then strain into a chilled glass over ice cubes. Garnish with lime slice.

Fiord

1 oz (30 ml) brandy
½ oz (15 ml) aquavit
½ oz (15 ml) orange juice
½ oz (15 ml) lemon juice
1 teaspoon grenadine

Pour all the ingredients into a cocktail shaker with ice. Shake well, then strain into a chilled glass.

Fruit Punch

1 lb (500 g) cherries, pitted
1½ cups sliced peaches
1 cup sliced pineapple
1 cup (250 ml) lemon juice
2 cups (500 ml) orange juice
½ cup sugar dissolved in 1 cup
    (250 ml) water

1 cup (250 ml) brandy
1 quart soda water
2 liters white wine
3 cups (750 ml) pineapple
   juice

Mix together the cherries, peaches, pineapple, lemon juice, orange juice, sugar water and brandy. Put into the punch bowl about one hour before serving. Add a large piece of ice and pour on the soda water, white wine and pineapple juice.

Ginger Brandy Cooler

1½ oz (45 ml) apple brandy
   (or calvados)
1 teaspoon ginger-flavored
   brandy
½ oz (15 ml) lemon juice
ginger ale
1 chunk preserved ginger

Pour the apple brandy, ginger-flavored brandy and lemon juice in a cocktail shaker with ice. Shake well, then strain into a tall glass. Add a little ginger ale and stir. Add ice cubes and garnish with preserved ginger.

Horse's Neck

1 lemon
2 oz (60 ml) brandy
½ oz (15 ml) lemon juice
1 dash Angostura bitters
ginger ale

Peel the lemon in one continuous strip. Put the peel in a tall glass leaving one end hanging over the edge of the glass. Fill the glass with crushed ice. Pour in the brandy, lemon juice and bitters. Stir well. Add a little ginger ale and stir again.

Kirsch Cola

2 oz (60 ml) kirsch
½ lemon
cola

Pour the kirsch into a tall glass over ice cubes. Squeeze the half lemon over the glass, then drop it in. Fill with cola and stir well.

Kirsch Rickey

1½ oz (45 ml) kirsch
¼ lemon
soda water
3 fresh pitted cherries

Pour the kirsch into a tall glass with ice cubes. Squeeze the lemon into the glass, then drop it in. Fill with soda water and stir. Garnish with fresh cherries.

Lady

1½ oz (45 ml) brandy
½ oz (15 ml) Benedictine
½ oz (15 ml) orange juice
½ slice orange

Mix the brandy, Benedictine and orange juice in a cocktail shaker with ice. Shake well, then strain into a chilled glass over ice cubes. Garnish with orange slice.

Kirsch Mist

2 oz (60 ml) kirsch
crushed ice

Put the finely crushed ice into a glass and pour the kirsch over it.

MacBrandy

1½ oz (45 ml) brandy
1 oz (30 ml) apple juice
1½ teaspoons lemon juice
1 slice lemon

Pour the brandy, apple juice and lemon juice into a cocktail shaker with ice.
Shake well, then strain into a chilled glass. Garnish with lemon slice.

Madeira and Brandy

1 oz (30 ml) brandy
1 oz (30 ml) Madeira
½ oz (15 ml) dry vermouth
lemon peel

Stir the brandy, Madeira and vermouth with ice. Strain into a chilled glass with ice
cubes. Twist the lemon peel over the glass, then drop it in.

Manchester

1 oz (30 ml) apple brandy
  (calvados or applejack)
½ oz (15 ml)
  apricot-flavored brandy
1 oz (30 ml) lemon juice
1 teaspoon grenadine
1 dash bitters

Pour all the ingredients into a cocktail shaker with ice. Shake well, then pour into a chilled glass.

Matisse

1½ oz (45 ml) cognac
½ oz (15 ml) Dubonnet
½ oz (15 ml) lemon juice
1 teaspoon sugar
orange peel

Pour the cognac, Dubonnet, lemon juice and sugar into a cocktail shaker with ice. Shake well, then strain into a chilled glass. Twist the orange peel above the glass, then drop it in.

Montgomery

2 oz (60 ml) brandy
½ oz (15 ml) lemon juice
1 teaspoon curacao
½ teaspoon sugar
orange peel

Pour the brandy, lemon juice, curacao and sugar into a cocktail shaker with ice. Shake well, then strain into a chilled sugar-frosted glass. Twist the orange peel above the glass, then drop it in.

Patrician

1½ oz (45 ml) brandy
1½ oz (45 ml) Dubonnet
½ teaspoon Pernod

Pour the brandy, Dubonnet and Pernod into a cocktail shaker with ice. Shake well, then strain into a chilled glass.

Peach Brandy Cooler

2 oz (60 ml) brandy
½ oz (15 ml) peach-flavored
   brandy
½ oz (15 ml) lemon juice
1 teaspoon sugar
soda water
1 slice peach

Put the brandy, peach-flavored brandy, lemon juice and sugar into a cocktail shaker with ice. Shake well, then strain into a tall glass over ice cubes. Add soda water and stir. Garnish with peach slice.

Pine-apple Cocktail

1½ oz (45 ml) apple brandy
1 oz (30 ml) pineapple juice
½ oz (15 ml) brandy
1 chunk pineapple

Pour the apple brandy, pineapple juice and brandy into a cocktail shaker with ice. Shake well, then strain into a chilled glass over ice cubes. Garnish with chunk of pineapple.

Plum Rickey

2 oz (60 ml) plum brandy
  (slivovitz)
¼ lemon
soda water
2 slices fresh peeled plum

Pour the plum brandy over ice cubes in a tall glass. Squeeze the lemon into the glass, then drop it in. Add soda water and stir well. Garnish with plum slices.

Plum Wonderful

1½ oz (45 ml) slivovitz
½ oz (15 ml) lemon juice
½ oz (15 ml) orange juice
1 teaspoon maraschino
  liqueur
1 teaspoon sugar

Put all the ingredients into a cocktail shaker with ice. Shake well, then strain into a chilled glass.

Polonaise

1½ oz (45 ml) brandy
½ oz (15 ml) blackberry
   liqueur
½ oz (15 ml) fino sherry
1½ teaspoons lemon juice
1 dash orange bitters

Pour all the ingredients into a cocktail shaker with ice. Shake well, then strain into a chilled glass over ice cubes.

Port-Brandy Freeze

1 oz (30 ml) port
1½ oz (45 ml) brandy
1 egg
1 teaspoon confectioner's sugar
⅓ cup crushed ice
cinnamon

Put the port, brandy, egg, sugar and ice into an electric blender. Whirl on low speed for 20 seconds. Pour into a chilled glass and sprinkle with cinnamon.

Prairie Oyster

1½ oz (45 ml) cognac
2 drops Tabasco
½ teaspoon Worcestershire
    sauce
½ teaspoon Angostura bitters
1 egg yolk
salt and pepper

Pour the cognac, Tabasco, Worcestershire sauce and bitters in a cocktail shaker with ice. Shake well, then strain into a chilled glass. Put the egg yolk on top without breaking it. Sprinkle with salt and pepper. Drink in one gulp.

Red Apple

2 oz (60 ml) apple brandy
1 teaspoon grenadine
15 ml (½ oz) lemon juice

Pour the brandy, grenadine and lemon juice into a cocktail shaker with ice. Shake well, then strain into a chilled glass.

Sidecar

1 oz (30 ml) brandy
1 oz (30 ml) Cointreau
1 oz (30 ml) lemon juice

Pour the brandy, Cointreau and lemon juice into a cocktail shaker with ice. Shake well, then strain into a chilled glass.

Sloe Brandy

2 oz (60 ml) brandy
½ oz (15 ml) sloe gin
1¼ teaspoons lemon juice
lemon peel

Pour the brandy, sloe gin and lemon juice into a cocktail shaker with ice. Shake well, then strain into a chilled glass. Twist the lemon peel above the glass, then drop it in.

Snow Apple

1½ oz (45 ml) apple brandy
½ oz (15 ml) lemon juice
½ egg white
1 teaspoon sugar
⅓ cup crushed ice

Put all the ingredients into an electric blender. Whirl for 15 seconds and pour into a chilled glass.

Steeplejack

2 oz (60 ml) apple brandy
   (calvados or applejack)
3 oz (90 ml) apple juice
3 oz (90 ml) soda water
1 teaspoon lime juice
1 slice lime

Pour the brandy, apple juice, soda water and lime juice into a tall glass over ice cubes. Stir well and garnish with slice of lime.

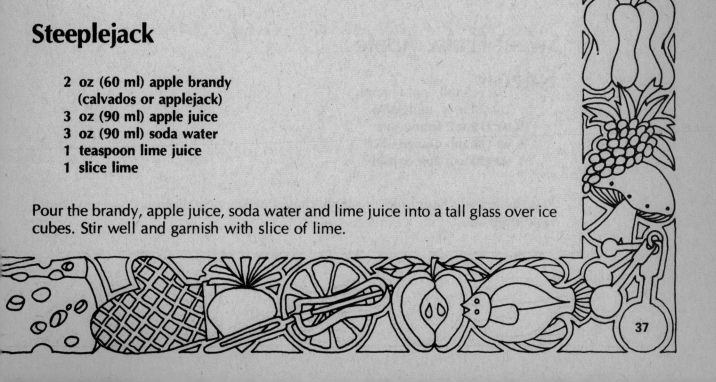

Stinger

1½ oz (45 ml) brandy
1½ oz (45 ml) white creme de
    menthe

Pour the brandy and the creme de menthe into a cocktail shaker with ice. Shake well, then strain into a chilled glass. (You may vary the ratio of brandy to creme de menthe. The less creme de menthe you use, the drier the Stinger will be.)

Sweet Brandy

½ teaspoon sugar
soda water
2 oz (60 ml) brandy
1 teaspoon Madeira
orange peel
nutmeg

Mix together the sugar and one tablespoon soda water in a chilled glass until the sugar dissolves. Add the brandy and Madeira. Add a little soda and mix well. Fill the glass with ice. Twist the orange peel above the glass and drop it in. Garnish with a sprinkle of nutmeg.

Sweet Fruity Apple

1½ oz (45 ml) apple brandy
    (calvados or applejack)
½ oz (15 ml) lemon juice
½ oz (15 ml) orange juice
½ teaspoon maple syrup

Pour all the ingredients into a cocktail shaker with ice. Shake well, then strain into a chilled glass.

Sweet Ginger Apple

1 teaspoon sugar
1 oz (30 ml) apple brandy
  (calvados or applejack)
1 oz (30 ml) ginger-flavored
  brandy
½ oz (15 ml) lemon juice
1 slice lemon

Mix the sugar with one teaspoon of water in a tall glass. Stir until dissolved. Add the apple brandy, ginger-flavored brandy and lemon juice and mix well. Fill the glass with crushed ice and garnish with lemon slice.

Sweet Stinger

1½ oz (45 ml) brandy
1½ oz (45 ml) sweet vermouth
1½ teaspoons Benedictine

Stir the brandy, sweet vermouth and Benedictine with ice. Strain into a chilled glass.

Swedish Glogg

1 quart claret
2 cups (500 ml) brandy
2 cups (500 ml) rum
10 whole cloves
1 cup almonds
1 cup raisins

½ cup currants
1 cup sugar
3 sticks cinnamon
grated rind of one orange
10 cardamom seeds

Put all the ingredients into a large saucepan and bring to a boil. Remove from the heat and cool a little before serving. Make sure each glass has a few currants, raisins and almonds.

Tokyo

2 oz (60 ml) brandy
1½ teaspoons orgeat
1½ teaspoons lemon juice
1 dash Angostura bitters
lemon peel

Pour the brandy, orgeat, lemon juice and bitters into a cocktail shaker with ice. Shake well, then strain into a chilled glass. Twist the lemon peel over the glass and drop it in.

Topeka

2 oz (60 ml) brandy
½ oz (15 ml) grapefruit juice
½ oz (15 ml) dry vermouth
1 teaspoon lemon juice

Pour all the ingredients into a cocktail shaker with ice. Shake well, then strain into a chilled sugar-frosted glass. (Wet the rim of the glass with grapefruit juice, then dip it in sugar.)

Fortifed Wines

Andalusia

1½ oz (45 ml) dry sherry
½ oz (15 ml) cognac
½ oz (15 ml) light rum
dash Angostura bitters

Mix all the ingredients with ice. Strain into a chilled glass and serve.

Brandied Port

1 oz (30 ml) tawny port
1½ oz (45 ml) brandy
½ oz (15 ml) lemon juice
1 teaspoon maraschino
   liqueur
1 slice orange

Pour the port, brandy, lemon juice and maraschino liqueur over ice in a cocktail shaker. Shake well and pour into a chilled glass. Add orange slice and serve.

Devil's Cocktail

1½ oz (45 ml) white port
1 oz (30 ml) dry vermouth
¼ teaspoon lemon juice
lemon peel

Pour the port, vermouth and lemon juice into a cocktail shaker with ice. Shake well, then strain into a chilled glass. Twist the lemon peel above the glass, then drop it in.

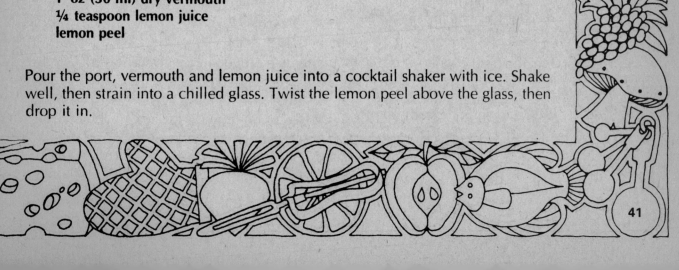

Granada

1 oz (30 ml) fino sherry
1 oz (30 ml) brandy
½ oz (15 ml) curacao
tonic water
1 slice orange

Pour the sherry, brandy and curacao into a cocktail shaker with ice. Shake well, then strain into a tall glass over ice cubes. Add tonic water and stir. Garnish with orange slice.

Hot Port Flip

3 oz (90 ml) port wine
1 oz (30 ml) cognac
1 teaspoon sugar
¼ teaspoon instant coffee

1 egg
1¼ tablespoons cream
nutmeg

Mix the port, cognac and sugar together in a saucepan. Heat, stirring constantly. Add the instant coffee and mix well. Beat the egg until foamy. Beat in the cream. Pour the port mixture slowly into the egg mixture, stirring constantly. Pour into a mug and sprinkle with nutmeg.

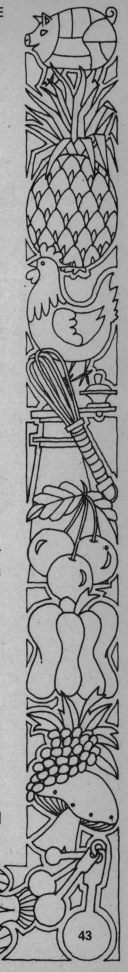

Port Cooler

    4 oz (125 ml) tawny port
    1 oz (30 ml) brandy
    ½ teaspoon sugar
    lemon peel
    orange peel
    mint leaves

Pour the port, brandy and sugar into a tall glass filled with crushed ice. Stir well. Twist the peels above the glass, then drop in. Garnish with mint leaves.

Sherry and Brandy Cooler

    1 oz (30 ml) cream sherry
    1 oz (30 ml) brandy
    ½ oz (15 ml) cherry liqueur
    1½ teaspoons lemon juice
    bitter lemon soda
    1 slice lemon

Pour the sherry, brandy, cherry liqueur and lemon juice into a cocktail shaker with ice. Shake well, then strain into a tall glass over ice cubes. Add a little soda and stir. Garnish with slice of lemon.

Sherry and Vermouth

    1½ oz (45 ml) dry sherry
    1 oz (30 ml) dry vermouth
    lemon peel

Pour the dry sherry and dry vermouth into a glass over ice cubes. Stir well and add the lemon peel.

Sherry Cooler

2½ oz (75 ml) sherry
1 oz (30 ml) brandy
½ oz (15 ml) orange juice
½ teaspoon sugar
1 slice orange

Pour the sherry, brandy, orange juice and sugar into a tall glass filled with crushed ice. Stir well and garnish with orange slice.

Syllabub

1½ oz (45 ml) medium sherry
1½ oz (45 ml) milk
1½ oz (45 ml) cream
⅛ teaspoon grated lemon rind
1 teaspoon sugar

Refrigerate all the ingredients for an hour. Combine in a bowl and beat well until frothy. Pour into a large chilled glass.

Gin Based Drinks

Amsterdam

1½ oz (45 ml) gin
½ oz (15 ml) lemon juice
½ oz (15 ml) orange juice
1 teaspoon sugar
1 dash Angostura bitters

Pour all the ingredients into a cocktail shaker with ice. Shake well, then strain into a chilled glass over ice cubes.

Apricot Gin

1½ oz (45 ml) gin
½ oz (15 ml) apricot liqueur
½ oz (15 ml) lemon juice
1 teaspoon grenadine
1 dash orange bitters

Pour all the ingredients into a cocktail shaker with ice. Shake well, then strain into a chilled glass.

Balmain

1 oz (30 ml) gin
1 oz (30 ml) dry vermouth
2 teaspoons Pernod
2 teaspoons lemon juice
1 slice lemon

Put all the ingredients except the lemon slice into a cocktail shaker with ice. Shake well, then strain into a chilled glass over ice cubes. Garnish with lemon slice.

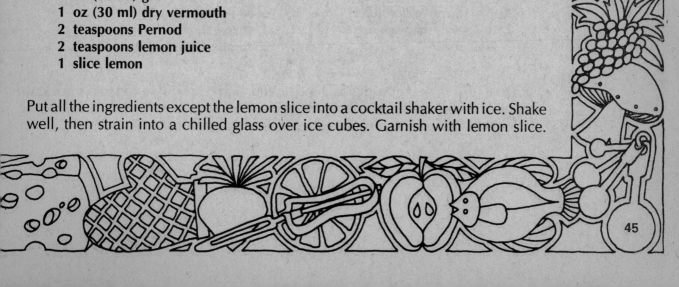

Bitter Martini

2 oz (60 ml) gin
½ oz (15 ml) dry vermouth
2 dashes orange bitters

Pour the gin, vermouth and bitters into a cocktail shaker with ice. Shake well, then strain into a chilled glass.

Blenton

1½ oz (45 ml) gin
1¼ tablespoons dry vermouth
1 dash Angostura bitters

Stir the gin, vermouth and bitters with ice. Strain into a chilled glass.

Bloomsbury Fizz

2 oz (60 ml) gin
½ oz (15 ml) lemon juice
2 teaspoons maraschino
   liqueur

1 teaspoon raspberry syrup
soda water
1 slice lemon
3 raspberries

Pour the gin, lemon juice, maraschino liqueur and raspberry syrup into a cocktail shaker with ice. Shake well, then strain into a tall glass over ice cubes. Add soda water and stir. Garnish with lemon slice and raspberries.

Blue Angel

1½ oz (45 ml) gin
½ oz (15 ml) blue curacao
½ oz (15 ml) lemon juice
1 slice lemon

Pour the gin, curacao and lemon juice into a cocktail shaker with ice. Shake well, then strain into a chilled glass. Garnish with the lemon slice.

Bougainvillea

1 oz (30 ml) gin
½ oz (15 ml) apple brandy
½ oz (15 ml) lemon juice
2 teaspoons sweet vermouth
½ teaspoon grenadine

Pour all the ingredients into a cocktail shaker with ice. Shake well, then strain into a chilled glass.

Bronx

1½ oz (45 ml) gin
½ oz (15 ml) orange juice
2 teaspoons dry vermouth
2 teaspoons sweet vermouth

Pour all the ingredients into a cocktail shaker with ice. Shake well, then strain into a chilled glass.

Caribbean Holiday

1 oz (30 ml) gin
½ oz (15 ml) dry vermouth
1 oz (30 ml) grapefruit juice
3 dashes orange bitters
1 slice orange
1 maraschino cherry

Pour the gin, vermouth, grapefruit juice and bitters into a cocktail shaker with ice. Shake well, then strain into a chilled glass over ice cubes. Garnish with orange slice and maraschino cherry.

Cherry Gin Fizz

1½ oz (45 ml) gin
½ oz (15 ml) Cherry Heering
1½ teaspoons kirsch
½ oz (15 ml) lemon juice
¾ teaspoon sugar
soda water
1 slice lemon
1 maraschino cherry

Put the gin, Cherry Heering, kirsch, lemon juice and sugar into a cocktail shaker with ice. Shake well, then strain into a tall glass over ice cubes. Add a little soda water and stir. Garnish with lemon slice and maraschino cherry.

Cherry Sling

1½ oz (45 ml) gin
½ oz (15 ml) cherry liqueur
½ oz (15 ml) lime juice

Pour all the ingredients into a cocktail shaker with ice. Shake well, then strain into a chilled glass.

Cloud Nine

1½ oz (45 ml) gin
½ oz (15 ml) dry sherry
½ oz (15 ml) cream
nutmeg

Pour the gin, sherry and cream into a cocktail shaker with ice. Shake very well, then strain into a chilled glass. Sprinkle with nutmeg.

Clover Club

1½ oz (45 ml) gin
1¼ tablespoons lemon juice
1 teaspoon grenadine
½ egg white

Put all the ingredients into a cocktail shaker with ice. Shake very well, then strain into a chilled glass.

Coffee Alexander

1 oz (30 ml) gin
1 oz (30 ml) coffee liqueur
1 oz (30 ml) cream

Pour all the ingredients into a cocktail shaker with ice. Shake well, then strain into a chilled sugar-frosted glass. (Wet the rim of the glass with coffee liqueur and then dip into sugar.)

Danish Gin

1 oz (30 ml) gin
½ oz (15 ml) dry vermouth
½ oz (15 ml) Cherry Heering
1½ teaspoons kirsch
lemon peel

Pour the gin, vermouth, Cherry Heering and kirsch into a cocktail shaker with ice. Shake well, then strain into a chilled glass. Twist the lemon peel above the glass and drop it in.

Dry Gibson

1 oz (30 ml) gin
1 oz (30 ml) dry vermouth
cocktail onion

Stir the gin and the vermouth with ice. Strain into a chilled glass and garnish with pickled onion.

Dry Martini

2 oz (60 ml) gin
1 teaspoon dry vermouth

Stir the pre-chilled gin and vermouth with ice. Strain into a chilled glass. May be served over ice cubes with a twist of lemon or an olive.

Edinburgh

1 oz (30 ml) gin
½ oz (15 ml) Drambuie
½ oz (15 ml) Scotch whisky
2 teaspoons lemon juice
lemon peel

Pour the gin, Drambuie, Scotch and lemon juice into a cocktail shaker. Shake well, then strain into a chilled glass. Twist the lemon peel over the glass, then drop it in.

Fino Martini

2 oz (60 ml) gin
½ oz (15 ml) fino sherry
lemon peel

Stir the gin and sherry with ice. Strain into a chilled glass. Twist the lemon peel over the glass, then drop it in.

Gin and Benedictine Sangaree

1½ oz (45 ml) gin
2 teaspoons Benedictine
2 teaspoons grapefruit juice
1 slice lemon
nutmeg

Pour the gin, Benedictine and grapefruit juice into a chilled glass. Add ice cubes and stir well. Garnish with slice of lemon and sprinkle nutmeg on top.

Gin Daisy

1½ oz (45 ml) gin
½ oz (15 ml) lemon juice
1 teaspoon raspberry syrup
soda water
1 slice lemon
2 mint leaves

Pour the gin, lemon juice and raspberry syrup into a cocktail shaker with ice. Shake well, then strain into a tall glass over ice cubes. Add a little soda and stir. Garnish with lemon slice and mint leaves.

Gimlet

2 oz (60 ml) gin
½ oz (15 ml) Rose's lime juice

Stir the gin and lime juice thoroughly with ice. Strain into a chilled glass.

Gin Alexander

1 oz (30 ml) gin
1 oz (30 ml) creme de cacao
1 oz (30 ml) cream

Pour all the ingredients into a cocktail shaker with ice. Shake well, then strain into a chilled glass.

Gin Daiquiri

1½ oz (45 ml) gin
½ oz (15 ml) light rum
½ oz (15 ml) lime juice
½ teaspoon sugar

Put all the ingredients into a cocktail shaker with ice. Shake well, then strain into a chilled sugar-frosted glass. (Wet the rim of the glass with rum, then dip into sugar.)

Gin Fizz

2 oz (60 ml) gin
½ oz (15 ml) lemon juice
1 teaspoon sugar
soda water
1 slice lemon

Put the gin, lemon juice and sugar into a cocktail shaker with ice. Shake very well, then strain into a tall glass over ice cubes. Add soda water and stir. Garnish with lemon slice.

Gin Mint

1½ oz (45 ml) gin
½ oz (15 ml) lemon juice
¼ teaspoon sugar
1 slice lemon
½ slice orange
mint leaves

Pour the gin, lemon juice and sugar into a cocktail shaker with ice. Shake well, then strain into a chilled glass over ice cubes. Garnish with lemon and orange slices. Tear the mint leaves in half before adding to the drink.

Gin Old Fashioned

¼ teaspoon sugar
1 dash Angostura bitters
2 oz (60 ml) gin
lemon peel

Stir the sugar and bitters together in a chilled glass until the sugar is dissolved. Add a couple of ice cubes and pour on the gin. Stir. Twist the lemon peel over the glass, then drop it in.

Gin Rickey

1½ oz (45 ml) gin
½ lime
soda water
lemon peel

Pour the gin into a tall glass over ice cubes. Squeeze the lime over the glass, then drop it in. Add soda and stir. Twist the lemon peel above the glass and drop that in, too.

Gin Rummy

1 oz (30 ml) gin
½ oz (15 ml) light rum
½ oz (15 ml) lemon juice
½ oz (15 ml) pineapple juice ·
½ teaspoon sugar

Put all the ingredients into a cocktail shaker with ice. Shake well, then strain into a chilled sugar-frosted glass. (Wet the rim of the glass with rum, then dip into sugar.)

Gin Sour

1½ oz (45 ml) gin
½ oz (15 ml) lemon juice
2 teaspoons orange juice
1 teaspoon sugar
½ slice orange
1 maraschino cherry

Put the gin, lemon juice, orange juice and sugar into a cocktail shaker with ice. Shake very well, then strain into a chilled glass. Garnish with slice of orange and maraschino cherry.

Golden Gin

1½ oz (45 ml) gin
1 oz (30 ml) orange juice
½ oz (15 ml) lemon juice
ginger ale
1 slice orange

Pour the gin, orange juice and lemon juice into a cocktail shaker with ice. Shake well, then strain into a tall glass over ice cubes. Add a little ginger ale and stir. Garnish with orange slice.

Green Demon

1½ oz (45 ml) gin
½ oz (15 ml) lime juice
2 teaspoons green creme de menthe
2 sprigs mint

Pour the gin, lime juice and creme de menthe in a cocktail shaker with ice. Shake well, then strain into a chilled glass over ice cubes. Tear the mint leaves in half before adding to the glass.

Hullabaloo

2 oz (60 ml) gin
½ teaspoon Angostura bitters
½ oz (15 ml) lime juice
¾ teaspoon sugar
soda water

Put the gin, bitters, lime juice and sugar into a cocktail shaker with ice. Shake well, then strain into a tall glass over ice cubes. Add soda and stir.

Joker

1½ oz (45 ml) gin
½ oz (15 ml) lemon juice
½ teaspoon sugar
2 dashes Angostura bitters
lemon peel

Put the gin, lemon juice, sugar and bitters into a cocktail shaker with ice. Shake well, then strain into a chilled glass. Twist the lemon peel over the glass, then drop it in.

Little Mary Sunshine

4 oz (125 ml) fresh orange
  juice
1½ oz (45 ml) gin
½ oz (15 ml) cherry liqueur
ginger ale
1 slice orange

Mix together the orange juice, gin and cherry liqueur in a tall glass. Add ice cubes and ginger ale. Stir. Garnish with orange slice.

Louisiana Gin Fizz

2 oz (60 ml) gin
1 oz (30 ml) lemon juice
½ egg white
2 teaspoons cream

1½ teaspoons sugar
soda water
1 slice lemon

Put the gin, lemon juice, egg white, cream and sugar into a cocktail shaker with ice. Shake well, then strain into a tall glass over ice cubes. Add soda water and stir. Garnish with lemon slice.

Madrid

1 oz (30 ml) gin
½ oz (15 ml) fino sherry
½ oz (15 ml) orange juice
½ oz (15 ml) lemon juice
¼ teaspoon sugar

Put all the ingredients into a cocktail shaker with ice. Shake well, then strain into a chilled sugar-frosted glass. (Wet the rim of the glass with sherry and dip into sugar.)

Marsala Martini

1 oz (30 ml) gin
1 oz (30 ml) dry vermouth
1 oz (30 ml) dry marsala
lemon peel

Stir the gin, vermouth and marsala with ice. Strain into a chilled glass. Twist the lemon peel over the glass, then drop it in.

Martini

2 oz (60 ml) gin
1½ teaspoons dry vermouth

Stir the pre-chilled gin and vermouth with ice. Strain into a chilled glass. May be served over ice cubes with a twist of lemon or an olive.

Mellow Yellow

1½ oz (45 ml) gin
½ oz (15 ml) grapefruit
2 teaspoons lemon juice
2 teaspoons yellow
   Chartreuse

Pour all the ingredients into a cocktail shaker with ice. Shake well, then strain into a chilled glass.

Miami

1½ oz (45 ml) orange juice
½ oz (15 ml) gin
2 teaspoons kirsch
2 teaspoons Triple Sec
1 teaspoon lemon juice

Pour all the ingredients into a cocktail shaker with ice. Shake well, then strain into a chilled glass.

Mint Alexander

1 oz (30 ml) gin
1 oz (30 ml) creme de menthe
1 oz (30 ml) cream

Pour all the ingredients into a cocktail shaker with ice. Shake well, then strain into a chilled glass.

Mint Collins

2 oz (60 ml) gin
3 large mint leaves
½ oz (15 ml) lemon juice
¾ teaspoon sugar

½ cup crushed ice
soda water
1 slice lemon

Put the gin, mint leaves, lemon juice, sugar and ice into an electric blender. Whirl on high speed for 15 seconds. Pour into a tall glass. Add a little soda and garnish with the lemon slice.

Mint Punch

1 cup (250 ml) lemon juice
4 cups (1 quart) pineapple juice
2 cups (500 ml) fresh grapefruit juice

⅔ cup confectioner's sugar
4 oz (125 ml) gin
2 oz (60 ml) creme de menthe
mint leaves

Mix together the lemon juice, pineapple juice, grapefruit juice and sugar. Mix well. Add the gin and creme de menthe and pour into a large pitcher with ice. Garnish with mint leaves.

Orange Blossom

2 oz (60 ml) gin
1½ oz (45 ml) orange juice
½ slice orange

Pour the gin and orange juice into a cocktail shaker with ice. Shake well, then strain into a chilled sugar-frosted glass. Garnish with orange slice. (Wet the rim of the glass with orange juice, then dip into sugar.)

Orange Blossom Fizz

1½ oz (45 ml) gin
2 oz (60 ml) orange juice
½ oz (15 ml) curacao
½ oz (15 ml) lemon juice
⅓ cup crushed ice
½ slice orange

Put the gin, orange juice, curacao, lemon juice and ice into an electric blender. Whirl for 10 seconds. Pour into a chilled glass. Garnish with orange slice.

Pernod Martini

2 oz (60 ml) gin
½ oz (15 ml) dry vermouth
¼ teaspoon Pernod

Stir the gin, vermouth and Pernod well with ice. Strain into a chilled glass.

Pink Elephant

2 oz (60 ml) gin or vodka
2½ oz (75 ml) lime juice
1 oz (30 ml) grenadine
1 egg white
1 cup crushed ice
1 maraschino cherry

Put the gin, lime juice, grenadine, egg white and ice into an electric blender. Whirl on low speed for 15 seconds. Pour into a tall glass and garnish with the maraschino cherry.

Pink Gin

2 oz (60 ml) gin
2 dashes Angostura bitters

Stir the gin and bitters with ice. Strain into a chilled glass.

Pink Lady

1½ oz (45 ml) gin
1 teaspoon cream
1 teaspoon grenadine
¼ egg white

Put all the ingredients into a cocktail shaker with ice. Shake very well, then strain into a chilled sugar-frosted glass. (Wet the rim of the glass with grenadine and then dip it into sugar.)

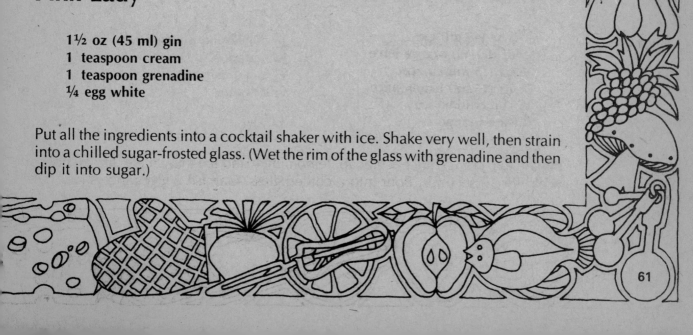

Princeton

1½ oz (45 ml) gin
1 oz (30 ml) dry vermouth
½ oz (15 ml) lime juice

Pour the gin, vermouth and lime juice into a cocktail shaker with ice. Shake well, then strain into a chilled glass.

Prunelle Alexander

1 oz (30 ml) gin
1 oz (30 ml) prunelle
1 oz (30 ml) cream

Pour all the ingredients into a cocktail shaker with ice. Shake well, then strain into a chilled glass.

Cantaloupe Cooler

½ cup diced cantaloupe
1½ oz (45 ml) gin
½ teaspoon Pernod
1¼ tablespoons cream
1¼ tablespoons lemon juice
½ teaspoon sugar
½ cup crushed ice
soda water

Put the cantaloupe, gin, Pernod, cream, lemon juice, sugar and crushed ice into an electric blender. Whirl at low speed for 20 seconds. Pour into a tall glass. Add a little soda water and ice cubes.

Sailors' Delight

    1 oz (30 ml) gin
    2 teaspoons rum
    ½ oz (15 ml) grapefruit juice
    2 teaspoons curacao
    ½ oz (15 ml) lemon juice

Pour all the ingredients into a cocktail shaker with ice. Shake well, then strain into a chilled glass.

Sake Martini

    2 oz (60 ml) gin
    ½ oz (15 ml) sake
    lemon peel

Stir the gin and sake with ice. Strain into a chilled glass. Twist the lemon peel over the glass, then drop it in.

St. George's Foe

1 oz (30 ml) gin
1¼ tablespoons green
    Chartreuse
1¼ tablespoons cognac

Pour the gin, Chartreuse and cognac into a cocktail shaker with ice. Shake well, then strain into a chilled glass over ice cubes.

St. Thomas

1½ oz (45 ml) gin
½ oz (15 ml) calvados
½ oz (15 ml) lemon juice
1¼ teaspoons sugar
lemon peel

Pour the gin, calvados, lemon juice and sugar into a cocktail shaker with ice. Shake well, then strain into a chilled glass. Twist the lemon peel above the glass and drop it in.

Scotch Martini

2½ oz (75 ml) gin
2 teaspoons dry vermouth
1½ teaspoons Scotch whisky

Stir all the ingredients with ice. Strain into a chilled glass.

Slalom

1½ oz (45 ml) gin
1 oz (30 ml) lemon juice
2 teaspoons maple syrup
1 dash orange bitters

Pour all the ingredients into a cocktail shaker with ice. Shake well, then strain into a chilled glass.

Sloe Gin and Vermouth

1 oz (30 ml) sloe gin
1 oz (30 ml) dry vermouth
½ oz (15 ml) lemon juice

Pour sloe gin, vermouth and lemon juice into a cocktail shaker with ice. Shake well, then strain into a chilled glass.

South Side

2 oz (60 ml) gin
½ oz (15 ml) lemon juice
1¼ teaspoons sugar
2 mint leaves

Put the gin, lemon juice and sugar into a cocktail shaker with ice. Shake well, then strain into a chilled glass over the mint leaves which have been torn in half.

Southern Gin

1½ oz (45 ml) gin
½ oz (15 ml) Southern
   Comfort
2 teaspoons grapefruit juice
2 teaspoons lemon juice

Pour all the ingredients into a cocktail shaker with ice. Shake well, then strain into a chilled glass.

Spinner

1 oz (30 ml) gin
½ oz (15 ml) Grand Marnier
1 oz (30 ml) orange juice
1 teaspoon lemon juice
orange peel

Pour the gin, Grand Marnier, orange juice and lemon juice into a cocktail shaker with ice. Shake well, then strain into a chilled glass. Twist the orange peel above the glass, then drop it in.

Strawberry Cream

2 oz (60 ml) gin
⅓ cup sliced fresh
   strawberries
1 oz (30 ml) lemon juice

2½ tablespoons cream
1 teaspoon sugar
soda water

Put the gin, strawberries, lemon juice, cream and sugar into an electric blender. Whirl on high speed for 15 seconds. Pour into a tall glass over ice cubes. Add a little soda water and stir.

Strawberry Gin

1 oz (30 ml) gin
½ oz (15 ml) dry vermouth
½ oz (15 ml) sweet vermouth
½ oz (15 ml) strawberry
   liqueur
1 large fresh strawberry

Pour the gin, dry vermouth, sweet vermouth and strawberry liqueur into a cocktail shaker with ice. Shake well, then strain into a chilled glass. Garnish with the fresh strawberry.

Strega Sour

1½ oz (45 ml) gin
½ oz (15 ml) lemon juice
2 teaspoons Strega
1 slice lemon

Pour gin, lemon juice and Strega into a cocktail shaker. Shake well, then strain into a chilled sugar-frosted glass. Garnish with lemon slice. (Wet the rim of the glass with Strega and dip into sugar.)

Summer Delight

2 oz (60 ml) gin
½ cup diced seeded
   watermelon
½ oz (15 ml) creme de cassis

1¼ tablespoons lemon juice
½ cup crushed ice
1 slice lemon

Put the gin, watermelon, cassis, lemon juice and crushed ice into an electric blender. Whirl on low speed for 15 seconds. Pour into a tall glass. Add a couple of ice cubes and garnish with lemon slice.

Summer Rose

1 oz (30 ml) gin
½ oz (15 ml)
   apricot-flavored brandy
½ oz (15 ml) dry vermouth
½ oz (15 ml) lemon juice
1¼ teaspoons grenadine
lemon peel

Pour the gin, brandy, vermouth, lemon juice and grenadine into a cocktail shaker with ice. Shake well, then strain into a chilled glass. Twist the lemon peel over the glass and drop it in.

Sunshine Gin Fizz

2 oz (60 ml) gin
1 oz (30 ml) lemon juice
1 egg yolk
2 teaspoons sugar

soda water
1 slice lemon
nutmeg

Put the gin, lemon juice, egg yolk and sugar into a cocktail shaker with ice. Shake well, then strain into a tall glass. Add soda water and stir. Garnish with lemon slice and a sprinkle of nutmeg.

Sweet and Dry Gin

2 oz (60 ml) gin
½ oz (15 ml) dry vermouth
2 teaspoons sweet vermouth

Stir the gin, dry vermouth and sweet vermouth with ice. Strain into a chilled glass.

Sloe Gin Fizz

1 oz (30 ml) sloe gin
1 oz (30 ml) gin
1¼ tablespoons lemon juice
soda water
1 slice lemon

Pour sloe gin, gin and lemon juice into a cocktail shaker with ice. Shake well, then strain into a tall glass. Add some ice cubes and a little soda water. Garnish with lemon slice.

Sweet Gibson

1 oz (30 ml) gin
1 oz (30 ml) sweet vermouth
cocktail onion

Stir the gin and vermouth with ice. Strain into a chilled glass and garnish with a pickled onion.

Tom Collins

2½ oz (75 ml) gin
1 teaspoon sugar
1 oz (30 ml) lemon juice
soda water
1 slice lemon
1 maraschino cherry

Put the gin, sugar and lemon juice into a cocktail shaker with ice. Shake well, then strain into a tall glass over ice cubes. Add a little soda and stir. Garnish with lemon slice and maraschino cherry.

White Rose

1½ oz (45 ml) gin
½ oz (15 ml) orange juice
½ oz (15 ml) lime juice
1 teaspoon sugar
½ egg white

Put all the ingredients into a cocktail shaker with ice. Shake well, then strain into a chilled glass.

Woolloomooloo Wonder

2 oz (60 ml) gin
½ oz (15 ml) tomato sauce
½ oz (15 ml) lemon juice
1 dash Tabasco sauce

¼ teaspoon Worcestershire
  sauce
1 cup crushed ice

Put all the ingredients into an electric blender. Whirl at low speed for 15 seconds. Pour into a tall glass.

Liqueur Based Drinks

Curacao Cooler

1 oz (30 ml) curacao
1 oz (30 ml) vodka
1 oz (30 ml) lemon juice

fresh orange juice
lemon peel
orange peel

Pour the curacao, vodka and lemon juice into a cocktail shaker with ice. Shake well, then strain into a tall glass. Add a couple of ice cubes and fill with orange juice. Twist the lemon and orange peels over the glass and drop them in.

Curacao Pernod Frappe

1 oz (30 ml) curacao
1 oz (30 ml) Pernod
1 teaspoon lemon juice
2 teaspoons orange juice

Mix together the curacao, Pernod, lemon and orange juice. Pour into a glass filled with crushed ice.

Grasshopper

1 oz (30 ml) white creme de cacao
1 oz (30 ml) green creme de menthe
1 oz (30 ml) cream

Pour the creme de cacao, creme de menthe and cream into a cocktail shaker with ice. Shake well, then strain into a chilled glass.

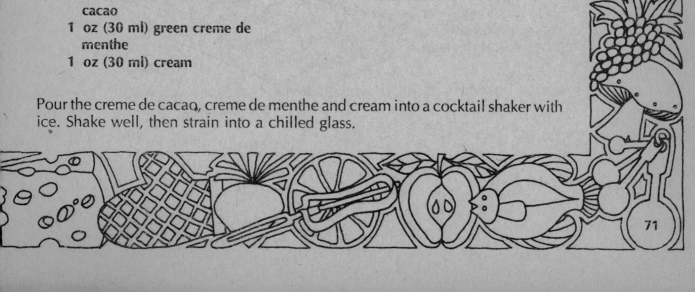

Mint Mocha Frappe

- 1 oz (30 ml) coffee liqueur
- 2 teaspoons white creme de menthe
- 2 teaspoons creme de cacao
- 2 teaspoons Triple Sec

Wet the rim of a glass with coffee liqueur, then dip it in sugar. Fill the glass with crushed ice. Mix together the coffee liqueur, creme de menthe, creme de cacao and Triple Sec. Pour into the glass over the ice.

Ouzo Milk Aperitif

- 1 oz (30 ml) ouzo
- 1 oz (30 ml) brandy
- ½ oz (15 ml) Triple Sec
- 4 oz (125 ml) milk
- cinnamon

Pour the ouzo, brandy, Triple Sec and milk into a cocktail shaker. Shake well, then strain into a chilled glass. Sprinkle with cinnamon.

Southern Peach

- 1 oz (30 ml) Southern Comfort
- 1 oz (30 ml) peach liqueur
- 1¼ tablespoons cream
- 1 slice fresh peach

Pour the Southern Comfort, peach liqueur and cream into a cocktail shaker with ice. Shake well, then strain into a glass over crushed ice. Garnish with peach slice.

Rum Based Drinks

Apricot Frappe

1½ oz (45 ml) light rum
1 oz (30 ml) apricot-flavored
  brandy
½ oz (15 ml) lemon juice

½ teaspoon curacao
½ egg white
⅓ cup crushed ice
1 slice orange

Put the rum, apricot-flavored brandy, lemon juice, curacao, egg white and crushed ice into an electric blender. Whirl for 15 seconds on a low speed. Pour into a chilled glass and garnish with orange slice.

Beach Bum

1½ oz (45 ml) rum
½ oz (15 ml) lemon juice
½ oz (15 ml) Triple Sec
½ teaspoon maraschino
  liqueur

Pour all the ingredients into a cocktail shaker with ice. Shake well, then strain into a chilled sugar-frosted glass. (Wet the rim of the glass with rum, then dip into sugar.)

Cherry Daiquiri

1½ oz (45 ml) light rum
½ oz (15 ml) lemon juice
½ oz (15 ml) cherry liqueur
¼ teaspoon kirsch
lemon peel

Pour the rum, lemon juice, cherry liqueur and kirsch into a cocktail shaker with ice. Shake well, then strain into a chilled glass. Twist the lemon peel above the glass and drop it in.

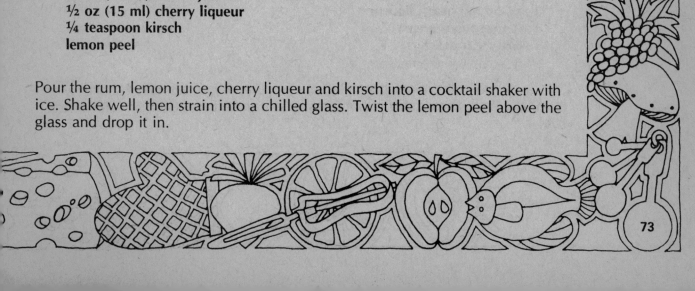

Chocolate Rum

1 oz (30 ml) light rum
½ oz (15 ml) creme de cacao
½ oz (15 ml) cream
½ oz (15 ml) creme de menthe

Pour all the ingredients into a cocktail shaker with ice. Shake well, then strain into a chilled glass.

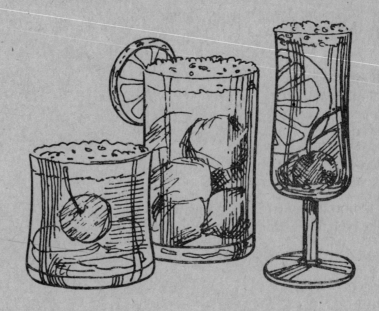

Daiquiri

2 oz (60 ml) light rum
½ oz (15 ml) lemon or lime
   juice
½ teaspoon sugar

Put all the ingredients into a cocktail shaker with ice. Shake well, then strain into a chilled glass over crushed ice.

Devil's Delight

1 oz (30 ml) light rum
1 oz (30 ml) brandy
1 oz (30 ml) Cointreau
1¼ tablespoons lemon juice

Pour all the ingredients into a cocktail shaker with ice. Shake well, then strain into a chilled glass.

Mexican Marvel

2 oz (60 ml) light rum
½ oz (15 ml) lemon juice
1½ teaspoons Triple Sec
½ egg white
½ teaspoon sugar
2 mint leaves

Put the rum, lemon juice, Triple Sec, egg white and sugar into a cocktail shaker with ice. Shake well, then strain into a chilled glass. Tear the mint leaves and drop them in.

Rum Aperitif

1 oz (30 ml) dry vermouth
1 oz (30 ml) light rum
1 teaspoon dark rum
1 teaspoon raspberry syrup
½ oz (15 ml) lemon juice
lemon peel

Pour the dry vermouth, light rum, dark rum, raspberry syrup and lemon juice into a cocktail shaker with ice. Shake well. Strain into a chilled glass. Twist the lemon peel over the glass, then drop it in.

Rum Apple Rickey

1 oz (30 ml) light rum
1 oz (30 ml) apple brandy
    (calvados or applejack)
¼ lemon
soda water
orange peel

Pour the rum and brandy into a glass over ice cubes. Squeeze the lemon into the glass and drop it in. Add a little soda and stir. Twist the orange peel over the glass, then drop it in, too.

Rum-Brandy Freeze

1 oz (30 ml) light rum
1½ oz (45 ml) brandy
½ oz (15 ml) lemon juice
1 egg yolk
1 teaspoon confectioner's sugar
⅓ cup crushed ice

Put all the ingredients into an electric blender. Whirl for 20 seconds on low speed. Pour into a chilled glass.

Rum Eggnog

1 oz (30 ml) dark rum
2 teaspoons sugar dissolved
   in 1 tablespoon water
1¼ tablespoons cognac

1 egg
2 oz (60 ml) cream
4 oz (125 ml) milk
nutmeg

Put all the ingredients into a cocktail shaker with ice. Shake well, then strain into a tall glass. Sprinkle with nutmeg.

Rum Punch

1 bottle Jamaica rum
6 oz (165 ml) peach brandy
2 cups (500 ml) lemon juice
1 cup (250 ml) orange juice
2 cups sugar

1 cup pineapple pieces
3 cups (750 ml) boiling green
   tea
strawberries

Mix together the rum, peach brandy, lemon juice, orange juice, sugar and pineapple pieces in a large bowl. Add the boiling tea and allow to stand overnight. When ready to serve, pour over a large block of ice in a punch bowl and garnish with strawberries.

Hot Buttered Rum

2 whole cloves
1 inch (2½ cm) stick of
   cinnamon
¾ teaspoon sugar

1½ oz (45 ml) hot light rum
½ oz (15 ml) hot dark rum
boiling water
1 teaspoon butter

Put the cloves, cinnamon stick and sugar into a mug with about 1½ tablespoons boiling water. Allow to stand for five minutes. Add the hot rum and 2 oz (60 ml) boiling water. Stir in the butter until it is dissolved.

Vermouth Based Drinks

Bittersweet

1½ oz (45 ml) sweet vermouth
1½ oz (45 ml) dry vermouth
2 dashes Angostura bitters
1 dash orange bitters
orange peel

Stir together the sweet and dry vermouth, Angostura and orange bitters with ice. Strain into a chilled glass. Twist the orange peel over the glass and drop it in.

Butterfly

1 oz (30 ml) dry vermouth
1 oz (30 ml) sweet vermouth
½ oz (15 ml) Dubonnet
1 oz (30 ml) orange juice

Pour all the ingredients into a cocktail shaker with ice. Shake well, then pour over ice cubes in a chilled glass.

Californian

1½ oz (45 ml) sweet vermouth
1 oz (30 ml) whiskey
2 oz (60 ml) fresh orange juice
1 teaspoon orgeat

Pour all the ingredients into a cocktail shaker with ice. Shake well, then strain into a chilled glass over ice.

Combo

2½ oz (75 ml) dry vermouth
½ teaspoon curacao
½ teaspoon sugar
¼ teaspoon Angostura bitters
1 teaspoon cognac

Pour all the ingredients into a cocktail shaker with ice. Shake well, then strain into a chilled glass over ice.

French Kiss

2 oz (60 ml) dry vermouth
2 oz (60 ml) sweet vermouth
lemon peel

Pour the dry and sweet vermouth into a glass over ice. Add a twist of lemon.

Plum Cocktail

1½ oz (45 ml) dry vermouth
½ oz (15 ml) cognac
1½ teaspoons prunelle
1 slice lemon

Stir dry vermouth, cognac and prunelle with ice. Strain into a glass over ice cubes. Add lemon slice.

Strawberry Vermouth Fizz

2½ oz (75 ml) dry vermouth
¼ cup sliced fresh
   strawberries
1 oz (30 ml) gin

2 teaspoons raspberry syrup
½ cup crushed ice
soda water
1 slice lemon

Put the vermouth, strawberries, gin, raspberry syrup and ice into an electric blender. Whirl for 15 seconds then pour into a tall glass with ice cubes. Add a little soda, stir well and garnish with lemon slice.

Vermouth and Triple Sec

1 oz (30 ml) dry vermouth
½ oz (15 ml) Triple Sec
1 oz (30 ml) gin
2 dashes orange bitters
lemon peel

Pour the vermouth, Triple Sec, gin and orange bitters into a cocktail shaker with ice. Shake well, then strain into a chilled glass. Twist the lemon peel above the glass, then drop it in.

Triple Treat

1 oz (30 ml) dry vermouth
1 oz (30 ml) sweet vermouth
1 oz (30 ml) gin

Stir well with ice, then strain into a chilled glass.

Vermouth and Bitter Lemon

1½ oz (45 ml) dry vermouth
1 oz (30 ml) gin
1 teaspoon raspberry syrup
1 teaspoon lemon juice
bitter lemon soda
lemon peel

Pour the vermouth, gin, raspberry syrup and lemon juice into a cocktail shaker with ice. Shake well, then strain into a tall glass over ice cubes. Add a little bitter lemon and stir. Twist the lemon peel over the glass, then drop it in.

Vermouth with Cassis

2 oz (60 ml) dry vermouth
1 oz (30 ml) creme de cassis
soda water

Pour the vermouth and cassis over ice cubes in a chilled glass. Add a little soda water and stir.

Vermouth and Maraschino

2 oz (60 ml) dry vermouth
½ oz (15 ml) maraschino
  liqueur
½ oz (15 ml) lemon juice
2 dashes orange bitters
1 maraschino cherry

Pour the vermouth, maraschino liqueur, lemon juice and bitters into a cocktail shaker with ice. Shake well, then strain into a chilled glass over ice cubes. Garnish with maraschino cherry.

Vermouth and Orange Juice

2½ oz (75 ml) orange juice
3 oz (90 ml) sweet vermouth
½ oz (15 ml) lemon juice
½ oz (15 ml) cherry liqueur
bitter lemon soda
1 slice orange

Pour the orange juice, vermouth, lemon juice and cherry liqueur in a cocktail shaker with ice. Shake well, then strain into a tall glass over ice cubes. Add a little bitter lemon and stir. Garnish with the orange slice.

Vodka Based Drinks

Bull Shot

4 oz (125 ml) chilled beef
   consomme
1½ oz (45 ml) vodka
1 slice lemon

Pour the consomme and vodka into a tall glass over ice cubes. Stir well and garnish with lemon slice.

Vermouth and Vodka Cooler

2 oz (60 ml) sweet vermouth
1 oz (30 ml) vodka
½ oz (15 ml) lemon juice
1 teaspoon sugar
soda water
1 slice lemon

Pour the vermouth, vodka, lemon juice and sugar into a cocktail shaker with ice. Shake well, then strain into a tall glass with ice cubes. Add a little soda and stir. Garnish with lemon slice.

Whiskey Based Drinks

Blended Whiskey

2 oz (60 ml) blended whiskey
½ oz (15 ml) Southern Comfort
¼ cup chopped fresh peaches
½ oz (15 ml) dry vermouth

1½ oz (45 ml) lemon juice
1 oz (30 ml) orange juice
½ cup crushed ice
1 slice lemon
1 slice orange

Put the whiskey, Southern Comfort, peaches, vermouth, lemon juice, orange juice and crushed ice into an electric blender. Whirl at high speed for 15 seconds. Pour into a tall glass and garnish with lemon and orange slices.

Coffee Eggnog

1 oz (30 ml) whiskey
1 oz (30 ml) coffee liqueur
1 egg
4 oz (125 ml) milk
1 oz (30 ml) cream
1 teaspoon sugar
½ teaspoon instant coffee
grated chocolate

Put the whiskey, coffee liqueur, egg, milk, cream, sugar and instant coffee into a cocktail shaker with ice. Shake for at least one minute. Strain into a tall glass and sprinkle with grated chocolate.

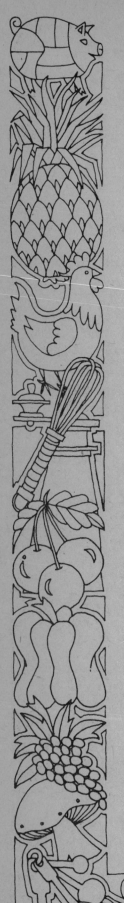

Dixie

1½ oz (45 ml) whiskey
½ oz (15 ml) Southern
    Comfort
½ oz (15 ml) lemon juice
½ teaspoon sugar
½ slice orange
1 slice peach

Pour the whiskey, Southern Comfort, lemon juice and sugar into a cocktail shaker with ice. Shake well, then strain into a chilled glass. Garnish with orange and peach slices.

Empire

2 oz (60 ml) whiskey
2 teaspoons lemon juice
½ oz (15 ml) Van der Hum
    liqueur
orange peel

Pour the whiskey, lemon juice and Van der Hum liqueur into a cocktail shaker with ice. Shake well, then strain into a chilled glass. Twist the orange peel above the glass and drop it in.

Good Friend

2½ oz (75 ml) Scotch whiskey
3 teaspoons honey
½ oz (15 ml) Triple Sec
4 oz (125 ml) milk
1 oz (30 ml) cream
¼ teaspoon grated orange
    rind

Pour the Scotch, honey and Triple Sec into a tall glass. Stir well until honey is thoroughly blended. Add the milk, cream and orange rind. Put into enough ice cubes to fill the glass. Stir well.

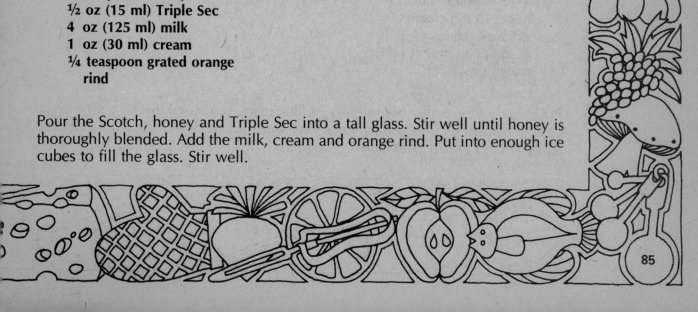

Irish Coffee

6 oz (165 ml) hot black coffee
1½ oz (45 ml) Irish whiskey
1 teaspoon sugar
sweetened whipped cream

Pour the coffee and whiskey into a warmed goblet. Add sugar and stir until dissolved. Top with a generous amount of whipped cream.

Lord Howe

1½ oz (45 ml) whiskey
1 tablespoon dry vermouth
1½ teaspoons Pernod
¼ teaspoon maraschino
   liqueur
½ oz (15 ml) orange juice
1 dash Angostura bitters

Pour all the ingredients into a cocktail shaker with ice. Shake well, then strain into a chilled glass.

Manhattan

2 oz (60 ml) whiskey
½ oz (15 ml) sweet vermouth
1 dash bitters
1 maraschino cherry

Stir the whiskey, vermouth and bitters well with ice. Strain into a chilled glass and garnish with the cherry.

Mississippi

1½ oz (45 ml) whiskey
½ oz (15 ml) unsweetened
  grapefruit juice
2 teaspoons raspberry liqueur
1½ teaspoons sweet
  vermouth.

Pour all the ingredients into a cocktail shaker with ice. Shake well, then strain into a chilled glass over ice cubes.

Mount Fujiyama

2 oz (60 ml) whiskey
½ oz (15 ml) port
½ oz (15 ml) lemon juice
1 teaspoon sugar
soda water
orange peel
1 chunk pineapple

Put the whiskey, port, lemon juice and sugar into a cocktail shaker with ice. Shake well, then strain into a tall glass over ice cubes. Add a little soda and stir. Twist the orange peel above the glass and drop it in. Garnish with pineapple chunk.

Mollymook

1½ oz (45 ml) whiskey
½ oz (15 ml) lemon juice
2 teaspoons dry vermouth
2 teaspoons sweet vermouth
lemon peel

Pour the whiskey, lemon juice, dry vermouth and sweet vermouth into a cocktail shaker with ice. Shake well, then strain into a chilled glass.

Mount Eliza

2 oz (60 ml) Scotch whisky
1 oz (30 ml) cherry liqueur
½ oz (15 ml) sweet vermouth
1 oz (30 ml) lemon juice
½ egg white
1 slice lemon

Pour the Scotch, cherry liqueur, vermouth, lemon juice and egg white into a cocktail shaker with ice. Shake very well, then strain into a chilled glass. Garnish with lemon slice.

Orange Whiskey

1½ oz (45 ml) whiskey
½ oz (15 ml) curacao
½ oz (15 ml) lemon juice
1 slice orange

Pour the whiskey, curacao and lemon juice into a cocktail shaker with ice. Shake well, then strain into a chilled glass. Garnish with orange slice.

Old Fashioned

½ teaspoon sugar
1 dash Angostura bitters
2 teaspoons water
2 oz (60 ml) whiskey
lemon peel
maraschino cherry

Mix together the sugar, bitters and water in a chilled glass until the sugar is dissolved. Fill the glass with ice and pour on the whiskey. Twist the lemon peel over the glass and drop it in. Garnish with cherry.

Paddington

1½ oz (45 ml) whiskey
½ oz (15 ml) lime juice
1 teaspoon sugar
1½ teaspoons grenadine
lemon peel
orange peel

Pour the whiskey, lime juice, sugar and grenadine into a cocktail shaker with ice. Shake well, then strain into a chilled sugar-frosted glass. Twist the peels above the glass and drop them in. (Wet the rim of the glass with whiskey and dip in sugar.)

Rear Admiral

2 oz (60 ml) whiskey
2 teaspoons lemon juice
1 teaspoon orange juice
1 teaspoon strawberry
  liqueur
1 dash orange bitters
1 slice orange

Pour the whiskey, lemon juice, orange juice, strawberry liqueur and bitters into a cocktail shaker with ice. Shake well then strain into a chilled glass. Garnish with an orange slice.

Rob Roy

2 oz (60 ml) Scotch whiskey
½ oz (15 ml) sweet vermouth
1 dash Angostura bitters
lemon peel

Stir the Scotch, vermouth and bitters with ice. Strain into a chilled glass. Twist the lemon peel above the glass and drop it in.

Rusty Nail

1 oz (30 ml) Scotch whiskey
1 oz (30 ml) Drambuie
lemon peel

Pour the Scotch and Drambuie into a chilled glass over ice cubes. Stir. Twist the lemon peel over the glass and drop it in.

Seaside

1 oz (30 ml) whiskey
1 oz (30 ml) gin
½ oz (15 ml) lemon juice
1 teaspoon sugar
3 mint leaves

Put the whiskey, gin, lemon juice and sugar into a cocktail shaker with ice. Shake well, then strain into a chilled glass over ice cubes. Tear the mint leaves in half before adding to the drink.

Sloe Whiskey

1 oz (30 ml) blended whiskey
1 oz (30 ml) sloe gin
½ oz (15 ml) lemon juice
1 maraschino cherry

Pour the whiskey, gin and lemon juice into a cocktail shaker with ice. Shake well, then strain into a chilled glass. Garnish with maraschino cherry.

Sour Red

2 oz (60 ml) blended whiskey
½ oz (15 ml) lemon juice
¾ teaspoon sugar
chilled dry red wine
½ slice lemon

Put the whiskey, lemon juice and sugar into a cocktail shaker with ice. Shake well, then strain into a chilled glass. Fill with red wine and stir. Garnish with lemon slice.

Tally Ho

1½ oz (45 ml) whiskey
½ oz (15 ml) kummel
1½ teaspoons lemon juice
2 teaspoons Rose's lime juice
1 slice lemon

Pour the whiskey, kummel, lemon juice and lime juice into a cocktail shaker with ice. Shake well, then strain into a chilled glass. Garnish with lemon slice.

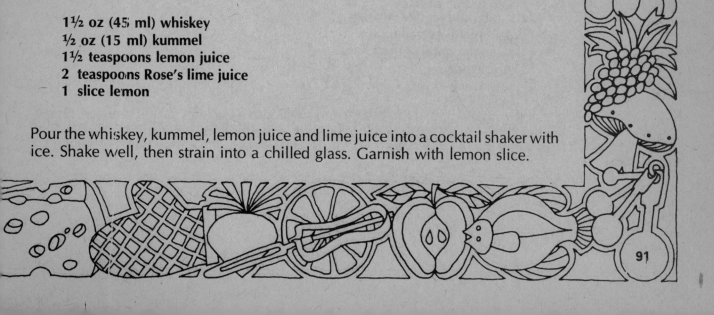

Whiskey and Curacao Fizz

2 oz (60 ml) blended whiskey
½ oz (15 ml) curacao
¾ teaspoon sugar
1 oz (30 ml) lemon juice
soda water
½ slice orange

Put the whiskey, curacao, sugar and lemon juice into a cocktail shaker with ice. Shake well, then strain into a tall glass over ice cubes. Add a little soda and stir. Garnish with orange slice.

Whiskey Sour

2 oz (60 ml) blended whiskey
1¼ tablespoons lemon juice
1 teaspoon confectioner's sugar
½ slice lemon
1 maraschino cherry

Put the whiskey, lemon juice and sugar into a cocktail shaker with ice. Shake well, then strain into a chilled glass. Garnish with lemon slice and maraschino cherry.

Wine Based Drinks

Champagne Cup

⅓ cup (85 ml) lemon juice
1¼ tablespoons confectioner's sugar
2 oz (60 ml) curacao
2 cups (500 ml) soda water

1 bottle champagne
ice cubes
strawberries
mint leaves

Pour the lemon juice into a pitcher. Add the sugar and stir until it is dissolved. Add the curacao, soda water, champagne and a few ice cubes. Pour into chilled glasses and garnish with strawberries and mint leaves.

Claret Punch

1 cup confectioner's sugar
2 cups (500 ml) soda water
2 lemons, thinly sliced
1 small pineapple, sliced
1 cup (250 ml) maraschino
  liqueur

4 bottles claret
1 bottle champagne
strawberries
ice

Mix together the confectioner's sugar, soda water, lemons, pineapple and maraschino liqueur. Allow to stand until ready to serve. When ready, pour the mixture into a large punch bowl. Add the claret and champagne. Put in a large piece of ice and garnish with fresh strawberries.

Miranda Cooler

2 oz (60 ml) dry white wine
2 oz (60 ml) very dry sherry
1 oz (30 ml) orange juice
1 teaspoon lemon juice
½ oz (15 ml) maraschino
   liqueur
dash Angostura bitters
soda water
1 slice lemon

Pour the white wine, sherry, orange juice, lemon juice, maraschino liqueur and bitters into a cocktail shaker with ice. Shake well, then strain into a tall glass over ice cubes. Add soda water and stir. Garnish with lemon slice.

Mulled Red Wine

250 ml (1 cup) boiling water
½ cup sugar
1 lemon, sliced
1 orange, sliced

10 whole cloves
1 cinnamon stick
1 bottle dry red wine

Mix together the boiling water, sugar, sliced lemon, sliced orange, cloves and cinnamon stick in a saucepan. Bring to the boil. Reduce heat and simmer for five minutes. Add the wine and simmer for ten minutes. Serve the mulled red wine in mugs.

Serves 6-8.

Raspberry Sauterne Punch

1 cup (250 ml) water
3 cups raspberries
2 cups sugar

1 cup (250 ml) lemon juice
2 cups (500 ml) orange juice
2 quarts sauterne

Put the water and raspberries in a saucepan and bring to the boil. Reduce heat and simmer for ten minutes. Press through a sieve. Add sugar and stir until dissolved. Chill. Add the lemon and orange juice and pour into a punch bowl over a large block of ice. Pour the chilled sauterne over the ice and garnish with fresh raspberries.

Index